Original title:
Knobby Quills Amid the Fae Stalk

Author: Swan Charm
ISBN HARDBACK: 978-1-80563-019-7
ISBN PAPERBACK: 978-1-80564-540-5

Where Chimeras Nestle in the Underbrush

In twilight's grasp, where shadows twine,
Chimeras weave in the bramble's sign.
With scales that shimmer, and eyes aglow,
They dance in whispers, where few dare go.

The underbrush sighs, a secret lair,
Where dreams entwine, and none are aware.
A flicker of tail, a flicker of thought,
In this realm of magic, the mundane is caught.

Their laughter echoes through crumbled vines,
In tangled paths, where mystery shines.
With hearts entwined in the moonlit night,
Chimeras play until morning light.

Nestled and cozy, in thickets deep,
They cradle the secrets that nature keeps.
For those who wander with open hearts,
Shall find the wonder where fantasy starts.

Legends of the Prickled Periphery

On the prickled edge where wild things dwell,
Legends arise in the evening bell.
With tales of courage and thorns that bite,
These whispered stories ignite the night.

In bramble and thistle, the twilight sings,
Of knights and dragons with shimmering wings.
The periphery holds what the heart holds dear,
Adventures await, for the brave and the near.

Each step taken into the unknown,
Breathes life to the legends that nature has sown.
With every prickle, a tale unfolds,
In the heart of the thicket, the magic beholds.

Brave souls weave through the shadows and light,
Chasing the tales that evade the sight.
In the spines of history, they find their place,
And in their own story, they leave a trace.

A Symphony of Stags and Spines

Through the forest's breath, like a soft refrain,
Stags roam in majesty, free from chain.
With antlers high, they reach for the sky,
In a symphony soft, they wander by.

Amidst the shady glens, the music flows,
Each rustle of leaves, where the river goes.
The spine of the world, both thorn and grace,
Echoes the harmony of time and space.

With the stars as their audience, they leap and bound,
In this quietude, magic is found.
Nature's orchestra plays through the night,
Where stags serenade in the moon's pure light.

Together they dance, a powerful sight,
In the heart of the woods, pure and bright.
With spines of the earth, and dreams intertwined,
A symphony echoes, both gentle and blind.

The Chronicles of Elfin Shadows

In the realms of whispers, where shadows sway,
Elfin footsteps dance 'neath the boughs of grey.
With secrets spun in the twilight's veil,
They weave their stories like an ancient trail.

The moon casts silver on their gentle forms,
Through canopies thick in the midst of storms.
Each flicker of light, a fleeting spark,
A chronicle penned in the hush of the dark.

With laughter like bells, through the mist they glide,
Elfin shadows hold the secrets inside.
In echoes of night, with each glowing trace,
A story of magic begins to embrace.

Tales of old world, of wonder and grace,
In shadows they linger, a hidden place.
For those who believe in the dance of the night,
Shall find in the dark the purest light.

Chronicles of Bristled Beauty

In the glen where shadows play,
Golden leaves twirl and sway.
A gentle breeze, a whispered sigh,
Nature's secrets cannot lie.

Among the brambles thick and wild,
Lies a charm, akin to a child.
With every step, the stories unfold,
Of ancient dreams and hearts of gold.

Bristled beauty meets dawn's embrace,
Caressed by light, time slows its pace.
A dance of colors, vibrant, bold,
Where memories shimmer and dreams are told.

In twilight's hush, the world now yawns,
The evening holds what daylight fawns.
Amid the thicket, whispers gleam,
Tales of magic weave through a dream.

So wander forth, dear soul, and seek,
The heart of nature, soft yet sleek.
For in this realm, your spirit flies,
Beneath the watchful, starry skies.

Whims of Wily Woodlands

In wily woods where shadows creep,
The laughter of the leaves runs deep.
A playful breeze weaves through the trees,
Whispers carried on fragrant ease.

Curious creatures dash and dart,
Each has a tale and hidden heart.
From glistening streams to rocks of moss,
Here in the wild, there's little loss.

The sun breaks free through tangled vines,
Dancing light where wonder shines.
A tapestry of green and gold,
Holds countless stories yet untold.

With every step, the forest sings,
An echo of forgotten things.
In this kingdom, rich and vast,
The present melds with echoes past.

So wander, seeker, through this land,
Palm the mysteries soft and grand.
Embrace the whimsy, let it find,
The hidden corners of your mind.

The Outpour of Thorny Whispers

Among the thorns, a secret sigh,
Melodies of the night creep nigh.
With every rustle, shadows blend,
An outpour where the dark extends.

Veiled in mystery, shadows call,
The wilderness weaves a silken thrall.
Each whisper spun from tangled roots,
Blossoms echoes in fierce shoots.

A cautionary tale flows like wine,
Of brambles sharp and paths entwined.
Yet hidden in the spines and scars,
Lie gems that twinkle like the stars.

Through thorny paths, the brave may tread,
Where gentle spirits softly spread.
And from the depths of what is torn,
New life arises, fresh and worn.

So venture forth, with heart afire,
Into the fray, heed your desire.
For every whisper, thorny, wild,
Holds the heart of nature, beguiled.

Echoes from the Grove of Echoes

In a grove where echoes lie,
Time drifts slowly, like a sigh.
Softly spoken truths arise,
Mirrored in the moonlit skies.

Beneath the boughs of ancient trees,
Secrets meld with evening breeze.
Each rustling leaf, a voice in tune,
With tales of the sun and the soft-spoken moon.

The air hangs thick with forgotten lore,
Whispers of ages, forever more.
From every trunk, a story shines,
The pulse of nature, in faded lines.

With every step, the echoes bloom,
Fragrant flowers dispel the gloom.
An invitation in every sound,
In this tranquil sphere, magic's found.

So linger here, where time stands still,
Absorb the magic, let it fill.
For in the grove of echoes clear,
The heart of nature draws you near.

Gnarly Postcards from the Enchanted

From forests deep, the whispers call,
With gnarly roots, where shadows sprawl.
Each postcard tells of secrets spun,
In the heart of where the wild things run.

A fluttering breeze with a hint of dreams,
Painted skies where the sunlight beams.
Colors dance on the edges worn,
Of tales that every leaf has born.

In hidden glades, the fairies sigh,
Where enchanted echoes weave and fly.
They send their love on winds so free,
To stir the hearts of you and me.

A charm that's wrapped in ivy's kiss,
In every fold, a moment's bliss.
The magic lies in the handwritten,
A world beyond the eyes unhidden.

So take this card, let wonder flow,
Embrace the tales of long ago.
For every stamp, a story brims,
Of dreams and laughter, soft and dim.

Whispers of the Timeless Thicket

In shadows where the wild things dwell,
The ancient trees weave tales to tell.
With every rustle, secrets tease,
Through tangled roots and cooling breeze.

A gentle hush, an ageless vow,
The heart of nature guides us now.
In thickets deep, where spirits play,
The timeless whispers lead the way.

The paths are hidden, the stars align,
With every step, their tales entwine.
In echoes soft, they sing of old,
Of stories lost, and legends bold.

The mossy stones, they watch and wait,
For every wanderer to contemplate.
In every breath, a memory formed,
Whispers echo, forever warmed.

Embrace the magic, heed the call,
In the thicket's heart, find peace for all.
For nature's voice is wise and clear,
In whispers soft, it draws us near.

Epiphanies in Prickled Canopies

Beneath a dome of twinkling light,
In prickled canopies, take flight.
Where every branch, a tale to weave,
In shadows deep, we learn to believe.

Above, the stars in silence shine,
A crumpled map of fate divine.
In secret nooks, the wonders sigh,
As dreams emerge and spirits fly.

The air is thick with magic's breath,
In every pulse, the dance of death.
Yet in the thorns, we find a way,
To bloom and shine, to dare, to say.

Revelations shine from every leaf,
In prickled paths, we find belief.
Epiphanies arise in the night,
Guiding wanderers with their light.

So wander on, let love unfold,
In every story, brave and bold.
The prickled canopies hold their secrets true,
With every step, they lead to you.

The Supply of Leafy Fables

In verdant glades where dreams are spun,
The leafy fables bask in sun.
Each story lingers in the air,
In every twig, a whispered prayer.

From emerald leaves, the tales arise,
In every flutter, wisdom lies.
The secrets held in nature's hand,
Await the heart that makes its stand.

The rustle speaks of the years gone by,
In leafy tomes that never die.
They tell of love and battles fought,
In every lesson gently taught.

The trails of moss will guide the way,
In the wild embrace where children play.
For every leaf, a story spins,
Of joy and laughter, loss and wins.

So gather round beneath the trees,
As stories dance upon the breeze.
The supply of fables endlessly flows,
In leafy whispers, the magic grows.

Fantasies of the Knotted Roots

Within the woods where shadows play,
In whispers soft, the dreams convey.
Each root a tale of olden lore,
A world beneath, forevermore.

The stars above in twilight's hue,
Reflect the hopes that once we knew.
With tangled vines and fragrant blooms,
A magic stirs within the rooms.

The wise old trees with arms spread wide,
Hold secrets close beneath their hides.
In knots they tie, our fates entwined,
In ancient woods where dreams align.

Twisted Reflections in the Grove

In moonlit glades where shadows sway,
Mirrors hold what night would say.
Through twisting paths of silver light,
The heart uncovers what feels right.

Each echo calls, a gentle tease,
The whispers dance among the trees.
A world where time itself stands still,
And thoughts unspool with quiet thrill.

With every sigh the leaves relent,
Revealing truths that were once pent.
A canvas drawn with tender care,
In twisted shapes, our souls laid bare.

The Enchanted Cradle of Nature's Keep

In nature's arms, we find our peace,
Where gentle winds and heartbeats cease.
Among the flowers' softest grace,
The world slows down, a warm embrace.

Beneath the branches, dreams take flight,
Stars emerge from the cloak of night.
With every rustle, every sigh,
Emotions rise, and spirits fly.

A cradle made of earth and sky,
In woven light where shadows lie.
Each whispered wish upon the breeze,
A bond with nature's mysteries.

Beacons of the Fabled Wild

In forests deep, where legends grow,
The hidden paths of magic flow.
With every step on mossy ground,
The pulse of life is all around.

With fireflies like stars in flight,
They guide the dreamers through the night.
The call of owls, a haunting tune,
Beneath the watchful, silver moon.

Each secret glen, a story's heart,
A wondrous place where wonders start.
From ancient tales, the wildly free,
Are beacons bright for you and me.

Sonnet of the Gnarled Woods

In shadows deep where whispers twine,
The gnarled woods guard secrets old,
With ancient trees that twist and bend,
And tales of magic softly told.

Beneath the boughs, where fairies play,
The leaves converse in gentle sighs,
While moonlight dances on display,
And echoes of the night arise.

The roots entwined with mystic lore,
A tapestry of dreams unfolds,
In every crevice, life does soar,
Enchanted visions yet untold.

Through tangles thick, the spirits roam,
Their laughter mingles with the breeze,
In this wild heart, we find our home,
Among the whispers of the trees.

So venture forth, let courage lead,
In gnarled woods, the brave may see,
A world where dreams and hearts both heed,
The magic that sets spirits free.

Scribes of the Hidden Groves

In secluded nooks where silence breathes,
The scribes of old with ink and quill,
Compose their tales among the leaves,
Their quiet work a boundless skill.

With parchment cradled on their knees,
They pen the songs of nature's grace,
Each stroke a dance with secrets teased,
In rhythm with the forest's pace.

Beneath the oaks, in twilight's glow,
The stories whisper, intertwine,
A symphony of ebb and flow,
As shadows soften, lines align.

The rustling leaves, their parchment bound,
Record the laughter of the glades,
In hidden groves where joy is found,
The magic of the world cascades.

So let us read these tales anew,
In every creek, in every bend,
For written there is nature's hue,
In hidden groves, the heart can mend.

Ethereal Whimsy in Natural Nooks

In corners where the sunlight gleams,
Ethereal whimsies waltz and sway,
Through blooming buds and babbling streams,
The magic of the earth at play.

With dappled light, the fairies spin,
And laughter dances on the breeze,
In every nook, where dreams begin,
Nature's wonders tease with ease.

From petals soft to towering trees,
Enchantments hide in every glance,
In vibrant hues, the spirit frees,
Inviting all to join the dance.

As twilight falls, the stars ignite,
Casting a glow on every path,
In natural nooks, hearts take flight,
Surrendering to joy's sweet wrath.

So wander forth in blissful cheer,
Embrace the whimsy, let it flow,
For in these nooks, the heart draws near,
To ethereal magic's gentle glow.

Luminescence of Bejeweled Stalks

In twilight's hush, the stalks alight,
With jewels that sparkle, shine, and gleam,
A symphony of colors bright,
Reflecting nature's vivid dream.

The dewdrops dance upon the blades,
In glimmering crowns they softly rest,
Each petal bold, in beauty cascades,
A playground for the sun's behest.

With whispers sweet, the blossoms sway,
Inviting all to pause and see,
The luminescence on display,
A moment's grace, a reverie.

As night descends, the magic swells,
The stars adorn the midnight sky,
In bejeweled stalks, the story tells,
Of nature's art that won't comply.

So take a breath, and linger long,
In this enchanted, vibrant show,
For in the glow, the heart belongs,
To bejeweled stalks, where wonders flow.

Legends Spun from Verdant Threads

In the glen where shadows weave,
Secrets stir and dreams believe,
Whispers of the ancient trees,
Guard the stories on the breeze.

Figures dance in twilight's glow,
Beneath the boughs where fairies flow,
Woven tales in emerald hues,
Crafting night with brooding muse.

Emerald threads entwine the sky,
Kisses soft like lullabies,
Magic lingers, softly spread,
Rustling leaves where hopes are bred.

Time stands still in nature's grace,
Hearts entwined in this sacred space,
Legends whispered, never told,
Are spun anew from threads of gold.

In this verdant realm we find,
The echoes of the old entwined,
A tapestry of dreams unfurled,
In whispered tones, we shape our world.

Melodies of Burly Sylvan Spirits

In the forest, strong and deep,
Where ancient giants hush and sleep,
Burly spirits guard the way,
Singing songs of light and play.

With each rustle, leaves applaud,
Echoes bounce on trails untrod,
Melodies of life unfold,
In the heart, their tales are told.

Gnarled branches sway in tune,
Underneath the watchful moon,
Joyous laughter fills the air,
In this realm, free from care.

They weave riddles with the night,
Stars dancing in sheer delight,
Burly spirits, stout and wise,
Sing of wonders, never lies.

In their arms, we find our peace,
Where the wild's sweet harmonies cease,
Each heartbeat, a gentle plea,
Together in this melody.

Vignettes from the Jagged Edge

On the cliffs where shadows crawl,
Vignettes whisper, beckoning all,
Rugged rocks hold tales of yore,
Echoes of the lost explore.

Salt-kissed winds and stormy skies,
Watch the sea where the seagull cries,
Each wave crashing, a fleeting glance,
Moments caught in a wild dance.

Horizon blends with dusk's embrace,
Time dissolving in this place,
Jagged edges, sharp and clear,
Hold the dreams we hold so dear.

Twilight drapes the world in gold,
Every secret, silent, bold,
Stories linger, sharp and bright,
In the jagged edge of night.

Heartbeats echo in the stone,
Each vignette whispers its own,
Tangled fate and windswept sighs,
Here, where the wild spirit flies.

The Scribe's Oak and the Dappled Light

Beneath the oak, a scribe shall rest,
With tales of magic, love, and quest,
Dappled light spills through leaves above,
Crafting words of wonder and love.

Ink from dreams upon the page,
Wisdom flows through every stage,
Stories linger, soft and bright,
In the dance of day and night.

Whispers weave through branches tall,
Each soft sigh a muted call,
Scribe's hands move with graced delight,
In concert with the fading light.

Time's sweet passage leaves a mark,
In the stories breathed in dark,
Every legend, softly spun,
Underneath the setting sun.

The oak stands firm through all it sees,
Guarding secrets in the breeze,
Written whispers in the bark,
Illuminate the world from dark.

Tales from the Burrows of Lore

In the depths where secrets lie,
Hidden paths of spark and sigh.
Whispers drift through mossy air,
Tales of wonders waiting there.

Beneath the roots, the magic hums,
A heartbeat soft, where dreaming comes.
With every twist of knotted vine,
Old stories glimmer, bright, divine.

Creatures tread with cautious grace,
Finding solace, a cherished place.
In burrows deep, the legends dwell,
In every shadow, a tale to tell.

Stars peek in through leafy shrouds,
Woven dreams in misty crowds.
The moonlight dances on their skin,
As whispers beckon them within.

So gather close 'neath ancient trees,
Let cool winds carry stories free.
For in each tale, a spark ignites,
A journey born on whispered nights.

Spines of the Forgotten Glade

In the glade where shadows creep,
Ancient secrets, dark and deep.
Thorns entwined in nature's hand,
Guard the thoughts of a magic land.

Moonlit paths of emerald green,
Twisted roots where hope has been.
Each spine a tale of long ago,
Of whispered dreams that ebb and flow.

Within the thicket, spirits prance,
In weathered warps of time's own dance.
Each prickly edge and jagged line,
Holds the echoes of the divine.

But wanderers tread with care and grace,
For not all paths lead to a place.
In the spines where shadows play,
Lie dreams forgotten, led astray.

So listen close to the rustling leaves,
In their whispers, believe, believe.
For in the heart of the glade's embrace,
Lie stories hiding without a trace.

Threads of Magic in Nature's Grasp

In the weave of twilight's veil,
Nature spins a wondrous tale.
Threads of gold and whispers bright,
Knit the fabric of the night.

Each blossom glows, a secret sign,
Telling tales of the divine.
Breezes dance on flowing streams,
Bringing forth the wildest dreams.

In every glade and sunlit grove,
The magic whispers, tempers trove.
With every rustle, every sound,
Life's soft heart can be unbound.

Crickets chirp in rhythmic cheer,
Nature's song is ever near.
From the tiniest dew-kissed petal,
To ancient oaks where shadows settle.

So linger long in mossy yew,
And let the threads weave into you.
For in each moment, pure and bright,
Magic thrives in simplest light.

The Dance of Whimsical Thorns

In midnight blooms where shadows play,
Whimsical thorns lead hearts astray.
A dance of petals, wild and free,
Entwined in nature's frolic spree.

Each thorny stem a secret holds,
Of dreams unspoken, tales untold.
Beneath the stars, the soft winds sigh,
Spinning journeys, lifting high.

The moon grants grace as branches sway,
In a ballet of twilight's play.
With every twirl, the world alights,
In the thicket's heart, the magic bites.

So heed the call of nighttime's throng,
As whispers blend in nature's song.
For every thorn that pricks and burns,
Also holds the dance, where joy returns.

Let laughter bloom amidst the thorns,
In playful jest, we greet the morn.
For in the wild, we find our way,
In the dance of life, come what may.

Gnarled Stems Beneath Starlit Canopies

In the hush of night's embrace,
Gnarled stems weave a hidden space.
Whispers dance in the cool breeze,
As lanterns flicker among the trees.

Crickets sing their ancient tune,
While silver moonlight bathes the dune.
Nature's secrets softly sigh,
Underneath the watchful sky.

Roots entwined in ancient lore,
Each twist reveals what came before.
Starlit dreams take gentle flight,
Guided by the cloak of night.

Beneath the canopies so wide,
Mysteries in shadows hide.
A world alive, yet calm and still,
Echoes of enchantment spill.

Among the trees where wonders blend,
The night whispers, secrets send.
Gnarled stems beneath the stars,
What stories lie, just who they are?

Enigma of the Twisted Bristles

Beneath a canopy of green,
Twisted bristles weave unseen.
Secrets curl in every twist,
Nature's puzzle, a hidden mist.

With every step, the forest speaks,
In rustling leaves, the mystery peaks.
Each bristle holds a story shared,
In silent whispers, nature dared.

Eerie shadows dance and sway,
As sunlight fades to end the day.
Thorny paths where few have tread,
Unravel truths long thought dead.

Nature's hands, deft and sly,
Plait the unknown, as ages fly.
Every bough, a riddle cast,
Enigmas deepen, shadows last.

Seek the truth in bristled throng,
In tangled beauty, right and wrong.
For those who wander, hearts ablaze,
Find magic in the twisted ways.

Wands of Wisdom and Wild Dreams

In glades where wild dreams take flight,
Wands emerge in twilight's light.
Crafted from both wood and thought,
Each spells a journey dearly sought.

With a flick, the world ignites,
Stars align, breaking night's plights.
Wisdom waits in whispered spells,
In shadows deep where magic dwells.

Wands of oak and willow weep,
Binding secrets they long keep.
Murmurs blend with the evening air,
Enchantments spark beyond compare.

Fractured dreams, a tapestry,
In hands of those who dare to see.
With every turn, a story blooms,
Lighting paths through shadowed rooms.

The heart of magic beats so strong,
In wands where foes and friends belong.
Hold them high, let bated breath,
Unravel wonders, dance with depth.

Shadows of the Mossy Thicket

In the heart of a mossy thicket,
Shadows shift, secrets picket.
Each branch tells tales of lore,
Where echoes linger evermore.

Sunlight filters through the green,
Casting dreams in soft sheen.
Moss carpets the earth with grace,
Enveloping time in its embrace.

Creatures stir in hushed delight,
Silhouetted by fading light.
They dance through the shadows, wise and shy,
Beneath the canvas of the sky.

Finding peace in tangled threads,
Nature's cradle, where life spreads.
In every nook, a tale unspools,
History weaves through mossy jewels.

So wander deep in thicket dim,
Where shadows play and lights grow slim.
In the depths of the forest's song,
Find the truths to which you belong.

The Poetry of Nature's Prickle

In the garden where shadows creep,
Every thorn yet holds a secret deep.
Beneath the bramble's kiss so slight,
Whispers of magic dance in the night.

A rose's allure, a touch of pain,
Life's beauty intertwined with disdain.
Prickle and petal in the moon's soft glow,
Each tale a gem from the earth below.

The rustling leaves in the tender breeze,
Tell stories of old, a timeless tease.
Nature's embrace, a paradox wide,
In every corner, wonder and pride.

Thorns mark the path where the brave have tread,
With courage born from the words unsaid.
In every sting, a lesson to find,
In nature's push and pull, we are entwined.

So walk with care where the wild things play,
Embrace the beauty in every fray.
For in nature's prickle lies a heart,
A world of enchantment, a work of art.

Tales Spun from a Leafy Vein

Beneath the canopy's emerald veil,
Whispers of wisdom weave out their tale.
Leaves rustle soft with a secret embrace,
Inviting you in to a magical place.

From roots that burrow in soil so deep,
Grow stories of ages that dreamers keep.
The echo of footsteps in time's gentle flow,
Each leaf a witness to all we don't know.

In shadows where sunlight barely creeps,
Lies the heart of the forest, where magic sleeps.
A blend of the ancient and newly born,
In whispers of green, a world reborn.

Twisting vines hold the moon's painted light,
Illuminating dreams in the heart of the night.
Breath of the earth sings a timeless song,
In leafy chambers where we all belong.

So listen with care as the breezes sigh,
For tales spun from nature will never die.
In the weave of the woods, where the wild is free,
Unravel the wonders that call to thee.

Dreamscapes of Twisted Flora

In realms where the orchids bend and sway,
Twisted flora beckons, come out to play.
Petals like whispers, soft as a sigh,
Dreamscapes of color, as time drifts by.

Where vines curl up toward the starry night,
Such beauty thrives, a surreal sight.
Lurking in shadows, a world unexplored,
Echoes of magic in each gentle chord.

Moss-covered paths lead to mystic dreams,
Where nature's heart pulses and gleams.
In this wild tapestry, lost and found,
Every twist tells stories profound.

With every petal that falls to the ground,
The earth whispers secrets, a wisdom unbound.
Twisted flora dances, a psychedelic trance,
Awakening spirits in a verdant romance.

So wander these paths where enchantment flows,
In dreamscapes of flora, let your heart pose.
For nature's own canvas paints visions anew,
In landscapes of wonder, waiting for you.

Starlit Barbs and Wistful Winds

Under a canvas of sprinkling stars,
The night unfolds with its wistful bars.
Barbs of the brambles, sharp yet bright,
Hold tales of love and lingering light.

Winds carry whispers from far-off lands,
Brush through the branches, caress tender hands.
A lullaby sung by the moon's soft glow,
In starlit embrace, the heart's secrets flow.

Each breeze that passes, a dream in disguise,
Bears stories of laughter, of tearful goodbyes.
Nature's own pen writes the verses so fine,
In the language of night, where the cosmos align.

Barbs of the roses, with beauty combined,
Reflects life's journey, both cruel and kind.
The starlight bathes every sharp edge in grace,
Illuminating paths each soul must embrace.

So let the winds carry you far and wide,
In the tapestry of night, let your spirit glide.
For starlit barbs and the wistful winds,
Hold mysteries deep where the adventure begins.

Chronicles Inked in Woodland Shadows

In whispered tones where spirits dwell,
The ancient trees weave tales to tell.
Soft moonlight dances on leaf and bark,
While shadows whisper secrets, stark.

With every rustle, a story spins,
Of star-crossed lovers, of cursed sins.
The forest breathes in moonlit sighs,
As legends stir beneath the skies.

Hidden paths where echoes roam,
These woods forever call me home.
A map of dreams in emerald lace,
In every turn, a realm we trace.

With ink of dusk, the night unveiled,
The heart of woodlands, where magic's hailed.
Each footstep soft, a cautionary tune,
Chronicles written by silvered moon.

So gather close, and listen well,
To the woodland tales that softly swell.
For in this place, where shadows play,
A world of wonders holds sway today.

Guardians of the Thorned Vale

In the vale where thorns entwine,
Guardians watch, both fierce and fine.
With eyes of fire and hearts of stone,
They guard the secrets, deeply sown.

Through whispered winds the stories rise,
Of battles fought 'neath stormy skies.
Each thorn a token of paths they've trod,
Woven tightly in nature's pod.

With each dawn's light, they rise anew,
Vows to the vale, forever true.
They shelter the timid, shield the meek,
In thorny embrace, they gently speak.

Through ages past and futures bright,
These guardians stand, in day and night.
A harmony born from toil and grace,
In their steadfast hearts, a sacred place.

So wander not where wild thorns twist,
Respect the vows that none should miss.
For in their strength, the vale's revealed,
Bound by the magic that's truly sealed.

The Fae's Secret in Gnarled Threads

In twilight glades where shadows creep,
The fae weave spells in silence deep.
With gnarled threads of ancient lore,
They craft their world, forevermore.

Hidden dances beneath the stars,
Twisted paths of old, like scars.
A flick of light, a chime of glee,
As laughter mingles with the free.

Each hidden nook, a treasure chest,
Where the heart of magic finds its rest.
In whispered tales, the fae confide,
Secrets of nature, tucked inside.

Through silver webs, their stories flow,
A tapestry of joy and woe.
In every bends and breaks, a chance,
To glimpse the fae in whimsy dance.

So tread with care where gnarled roots lie,
For in their midst, a truth may fly.
Open your heart, let wonder thread,
The fae's bright secret, gently spread.

Lore of the Twisted Spirit

In shadows deep, a spirit calls,
With whispers soft that gently thralls.
Its twisted lore, a haunting song,
Of where the lost and lonely belong.

Through fog and mist, the memories swell,
Of treasured times, of grief to quell.
A dance of echoes, a playful jest,
Reviving hearts from ancient rest.

In every sigh, the spirit sighs,
A bridge between the truths and lies.
With tales of old, they gently weave,
A promise kept for those who grieve.

In midnight's hush, we seek its face,
Finding comfort in its embrace.
A spark of light in endless night,
The twisted spirit, our guiding light.

So gather close, in dreams abide,
For in the stillness, our hearts confide.
With lore entwined in wisps of air,
The spirit's tale is yours to share.

Resilience Among Twisted Florals

In a garden where shadows dance,
Twisted blooms find their stance.
With petals painted by the sun,
They rise anew, though battles won.

Beneath the weight of stormy skies,
Each floral heart learns to arise.
Through cracks in earth, they reach for light,
Defying darkness, pure and bright.

Roots entwined, they hold their ground,
In silent strength, their hope is found.
Each leaf whispers tales untold,
Of warriors brave, and spirits bold.

Even when frost nips softly near,
Their vibrant colors persevere.
With every bud, a promise grows,
Resilience in the face of woes.

Twisted florals, bold and free,
Embody life's sweet poetry.
In every stem, a story weaves,
Of strength alive, as each heart believes.

Secrets Lurking Where Shadows Play

In corners dark where whispers creep,
Secrets hide and silence keep.
The moonlight shadows twist and turn,
Unravel tales the night may yearn.

Behind the trees, old legends sigh,
Mysteries that never die.
With every rustle, secrets flown,
In whispering darkness, truth is sown.

A lantern's glow, but fading slow,
Reveals the paths we dare not go.
Where shadows mingle, hopes entwine,
In every silence, a hidden sign.

Echoes of past, they weave their web,
In tangled thoughts, where fears ebb.
The heart, a compass in the fray,
Leads seekers on, where shadows play.

To find the light where darkness swells,
Unraveling all the hidden spells.
With courage strong, we face the night,
Embrace the secrets, find the light.

Melodies of Nature's Curved Edges

In forest depths where soft winds sigh,
Curved edges sing as they float by.
The leaves entwine in graceful dance,
Nature's rhythm in each chance.

Branches bend with gentle grace,
Melodies weave through time and space.
In every rustle, a story flows,
Of whispered dreams, and love that grows.

The brook's sweet laughter, a soft refrain,
Caresses stones, and soothes the pain.
Each note a brushstroke on the air,
Painting peace, a balm to share.

The sunset's glow, a canvas bright,
Curved edges kissed by fading light.
As twilight deepens, songs arise,
In every heart, the nature cries.

Harmony swells, the night descends,
In every pause, the magic bends.
Through every curve, embrace the sound,
In nature's melody, we are found.

Enchanted Thorns in the Twilight

Beneath the veil of twilight's mist,
Enchanted thorns twist and twist.
In shadows deep, a beauty rare,
A secret world laid stripped and bare.

With every rose comes pain's embrace,
Thorns guard the heart in hidden space.
Yet through the prick, a fragrance sweet,
In every hurt, a love can meet.

Cloaked in dusk, their magic stirs,
Mysterious songs that memory purrs.
Glimmers of gold, a spark ignites,
Among the thorns, the heart takes flight.

To wander here in fading light,
Is to find joy within the night.
With cautious steps, the brave will tread,
Where thorns and dreams alike are wed.

Among the thorns, a lesson known,
That beauty lies where courage's grown.
In twilight's arms, they stand and sway,
Enchanted thorns, where hearts will play.

The Playlist of the Woodland Wild

In the heart of the glen, where the shadows sway,
Whispers of creatures weave night into day.
Each rustle and chirp holds a melody true,
Nature's own symphony, forever anew.

The brook babbles softly, a rhythmic embrace,
While leaves dance and twirl in a wild, joyful race.
Crickets join in with their timeless refrain,
Every note woven in wood, silk, and rain.

By the old twisted oak, secrets are shared,
The spirit of nature must surely have cared.
With each gentle breeze, it sings loud and clear,
A playlist of magic that calls us near.

Under the starlit sky, the owls convene,
Their wise, watchful eyes keep the forest pristine.
Every rustling leaf tells a tale of its own,
In this woodland haven, we're never alone.

So gather your thoughts, let the music unfold,
In the whispers of leaves, let your heart be bold.
For in every small sound lies a world to explore,
The playlist awaits; let your spirit soar.

Secrets Inked in Leafy Traces

Among the green shadows, stories lay bare,
Each petal a diary, secrets to share.
In the dance of the wind, truths twist and twine,
Ink from the heavens, each drop a design.

Whispers exchanged on the breath of the trees,
A canvas of colors painted with ease.
From thorns and from thistles, beauty is born,
With each gentle rustle, a new tale is sworn.

Under the canopy, mysteries bloom,
Sunlight spills secrets in every nook gloom.
From berries to blooms, every shade holds a clue,
Awakening senses to wonder anew.

In the garden of dusk, shadows start to weave,
With delicate grace, every echo believes.
Nature records every sigh and embrace,
Ink in leafy traces, life's tenderest grace.

So listen closely to the hush of the night,
For secrets enshrined take on magical flight.
In the soft rustling leaves, let your heart trace,
Every story lived, in this sacred space.

Spirits of the Tanglewood Paths

In tanglewood shadows, where secrets thrive,
The spirits awaken, the forest alive.
Each twist in the pathway, a new tale unfurls,
Mysteries hidden in the darkened swirls.

Gnarled roots embrace as the night softly calls,
Echoes of laughter through the ancient halls.
Every turn taken is a step through the past,
In the whispers of breezes, the moments are cast.

Phantoms of the forest, in moonlight they dance,
Entwined with the shadows, lost in a trance.
Secrets of ages written in stone,
In the heart of the woods, we're never alone.

The fog gently lifts, unveiling the glen,
Where the spirits still roam, over and again.
They call to the wanderers, beckoning near,
In the tanglewood paths, their laughter we hear.

So wander these trails with your heart opened wide,
Find solace in nature, let the spirits guide.
For in every rustle, a story can start,
In the tanglewood paths, you'll discover your heart.

Enigmas Among Twisted Petal Tales

In gardens forgotten, where shadows conceal,
Twisted petal tales weave a delicate reel.
Fragrance of mysteries wafts through the air,
Each bloom holds a riddle just waiting to share.

Beneath the rich soil, where history sleeps,
Enigmas awaken, the silence it keeps.
Colors blend softly, in whispers they speak,
A language of nature, uniquely mystique.

By moonlight's embrace, secrets softly unfurl,
Petal by petal, a mystical swirl.
In the tapestry woven by darkness and light,
Every drop of the dew sparkles with insight.

From blossoms once cherished, now crumbled with time,
Their essence still lingers, a lyrical rhyme.
Each twist and each turn leads us deeper still,
In the heart of this garden, our souls find their thrill.

So delve into tales where the flowers reside,
Unravel the enigma, let curiosity guide.
For in every petal lies a story so grand,
Among twisted petal tales, here take my hand.

Whispers of Thorned Feathers

In shadows deep where secrets lie,
A whispered wind begins to sigh.
Feathers dark, like whispers cold,
Tell tales of hearts that dared be bold.

Once they soared on wings of grace,
Now they haunt this quiet space.
Beneath the thorns, the stories nest,
Of daring dreams and broken rest.

The moonlit path is lined with thorns,
Where echoes dance and hope is worn.
In twilight's hush, their secrets bloom,
In every shadow, every room.

Yet through the pain, the beauty grows,
In thorned embrace, affection glows.
So listen close, to what they share,
The whispers soft, that fill the air.

For every feather, lost in time,
Holds echoes of a whispered rhyme.
And in the dark, where dreams ascend,
The heart finds peace, a cherished friend.

Secrets of the Enchanted Grove

In the grove where wild things play,
Secrets hide beneath the sway.
Whispers of ancient trees arise,
Guardians of forgotten skies.

Mornings glow with dew-kissed light,
While shadows weave the tales of night.
Petals dance, the breeze a song,
In this realm where hearts belong.

Beneath the boughs of emerald dreams,
Magic flows in gentle streams.
Every rustle, a sigh, a grace,
In this sacred, timeless space.

The faeries flit, with laughter sweet,
They weave enchantments at our feet.
Join their circle, let go of care,
Feel the magic linger there.

As twilight cloaks the world in blue,
The grove reveals its secrets true.
With each starlit, silvery beam,
Awaken to the whispered dream.

Prickly Echoes in Twilight

As daylight fades, the thorns emerge,
In silent woods, where shadows surge.
Prickly echoes, sharp and bold,
Guard stories of a heart grown cold.

Each winding path is coarse, unkind,
Where tangled thoughts are left behind.
Yet in their grasp, there's something sweet,
A tender truth beneath defeat.

At dusk, when stars begin to spark,
Whispers rise from every dark.
Cloaked in night, a haunting call,
The prickly echoes guide us all.

For in the twilight's dusky veil,
Beauty blooms where shadows sail.
What seems a curse may yet redeem,
The heart that dares to chase a dream.

So walk the path where thorns entwine,
And find the joy in every sign.
In prickly spaces, love does dwell,
A whispered truth, an echoed spell.

Sylvan Spine and Moonlit Dance

In forests deep, where shadows play,
A sylvan spine leads hearts astray.
Beneath the stars, they twirl and spin,
In moonlit dances, dreams begin.

The leaves, like whispers, softly sway,
In the magic of the night's ballet.
Nature holds her breath in trance,
As woodland creatures join the dance.

With gentle steps, the silence breaks,
As every heart in rhythm wakes.
In harmony, they twist, they turn,
For every soul, a match to burn.

The moon, a watchful eye above,
Illuminates the steps of love.
In sylvan light, all fears rescind,
As dreams and nature's hearts are twinned.

So let the dance of shadows flow,
In every heart, let passions grow.
For in this night, under the skies,
We find our strength, we find the wise.

Mystical Gnarls Beneath the Moon

Under the glow of silver light,
Whispers of magic take their flight.
Gnarls of wisdom, ancient trees,
Guard secrets carried by the breeze.

Riddles wrapped in twilight's hue,
Shadows dance as dreams come true.
In every twist, a tale is spun,
Mysteries woven, one by one.

Beneath the stars, the night unfurls,
With every sigh, the magic swirls.
In darkened corners, echoes gleam,
A world enchanted, a dreamer's dream.

The gnarls stand watch, steadfast and wise,
Under the watchful, knowing skies.
Beneath their roots, enchantments creep,
A symphony that won't let sleep.

So wander close, let wonder be,
In moonlit realms, we find the key.
For in each gnarled, twisting branch,
Lies the heart of a hidden chance.

Elegance in Nature's Spiky Veil

Amidst the thorns a beauty lies,
A tapestry of greens and sighs.
Each spiky leaf, a guarded tale,
Of nature's grace beneath the veil.

The blooms arise, defiant, bright,
In fields where shadows meld with light.
Honeyed scents on breezes whirl,
Awakening the quiet pearl.

Emerald wonders intertwine,
In harmony, they twist and shine.
Through tangled paths, the heart must wade,
To dance with thorns in sunlight's shade.

With every step, a story told,
Of hopeful dreams and joys unfold.
In nature's grasp, elegance speaks,
Through prickly shells, the heart still seeks.

So pause and breathe this vibrant air,
In spiky realms, find solace there.
For beauty waits in every glance,
In nature's weave, we find our chance.

Thickets of Curiosity Awaken

In tangled woods where whispers grow,
Curiosity starts to flow.
Through bramble thick and shadows deep,
Awake the secrets they do keep.

Branches twist, a playful game,
Inviting souls to seek the same.
What lies beyond this leafy guard?
A treasure found, or dreams left scarred?

In the thicket, hearts explore,
With every step, they long for more.
Questions bloom like vibrant flowers,
Beneath the weight of leafy towers.

Where the wild things breathe and sigh,
Each rustle sings a lullaby.
In the thickets, fears unwind,
Curiosity, a bold heart's kind.

So venture forth, let wonders call,
Through tangled paths, you'll find them all.
In nature's spine, let spirit soar,
For curiosity opens every door.

Glimmers of Grit in the Fairie's Realm

In twilight's hush, the fairies play,
Through realms of mist where dreams hold sway.
Glimmers of grit in laughter weave,
A magic spun that few believe.

With twinkling lights, the stories twine,
Wonders crafted from pure design.
Each shimmer bright, a spark of will,
In every heart, a magic thrill.

They dance on petals, soft and rare,
With courage bold, a tender care.
Through trials faced in shadowed glades,
Their grit endures, a truth that wades.

For in this realm of fleeting grace,
Strength blooms softly in the chase.
With every thread, their spirits rise,
Filling the night with hopeful sighs.

So seek the glimmers, find your way,
Through fairie paths where dreams can sway.
In the twinkling light, embrace your fight,
For every grit shines pure and bright.

Whispers of Thorny Secrets

In the shadows where secrets blend,
Whispers dance on the autumn wind.
Thorns entwined in a lover's grasp,
Tales of old, in silence they clasp.

Moonlight spills like a silver stream,
Casting shadows where dreamers dream.
Each thorn a mark, a story untold,
Of love and loss, of courage bold.

Through brambles thick, the heart must roam,
Seeking solace, a place called home.
The secrets held in the forest deep,
Guarded wide where the wild things sleep.

Every sigh of the nightingale's song,
Echoes where the thorny vines throng.
In the hush of twilight's gentle schemes,
Even thorns nurture the tenderest dreams.

So tread lightly where shadows sweep,
For in their depths, the secrets seep.
A world awaits, both fierce and sweet,
In whispers of thorn, our hearts shall meet.

Enchanted Prickles of the Glade

In a glade where wildflowers bend,
Prickles dance with the breeze, my friend.
Nature's magic, in colors bright,
Whirls and twirls in the fading light.

Each petal's touch, a soft embrace,
Among the thorns, a charming race.
Starlit whispers weave through the air,
As creatures gather without a care.

A prickle here, a shimmer there,
Dreams entwined in the evening's glare.
Every rustle tells a tale anew,
Of brave little hearts and skies so blue.

As dusk descends, the shadows play,
With prickles soft leading the way.
In this moment, all worries cease,
Finding solace, a perfect peace.

So let the glade's enchantment soar,
With prickles and whispers forevermore.
In the heart of the wild, let us sway,
For in this magic, we find our way.

The Woodland's Quirky Dancers

In the woodland's embrace, they twirl,
Quirky dancers, a whirling swirl.
Beneath the boughs, where secrets delight,
Each prickle a spark in the soft moonlight.

With laughter that springs from the earth,
Their revelry sparks with endless mirth.
From ferns to blossoms, they leap and twine,
In a festival bold, so divine.

The fireflies join in, a shimmering crew,
Creating lanterns in hues of blue.
Every step leaves a story anew,
In this dance where the wild things grew.

Amongst the thorns, they waltz and glide,
Frogs croak softly, the trees abide.
As the night holds its breath, hearts entwine,
Dancers weave dreams in a cadence so fine.

So come join the woodland's enchanting fest,
Where quirky hearts find their joyous rest.
In the rhythm of nature, let's prance and prickle,
In every step, let our spirits tickle.

Shadows Wreathed in Prickly Light

In the twilight where shadows loom,
Prickly light begins to bloom.
Softly woven in the dark,
Mysterious whispers leave a mark.

The stars above twinkle with glee,
As shadows dance 'neath the ancient tree.
Every prickle glistens with stories spun,
Of battles fought and love that won.

Through the thorns, the night reveals,
A tapestry of what time steals.
The stillness hums with magic bright,
As dreams emerge from the calming night.

Wreathed in nerves, yet cloaked in peace,
Every rustle brings a sweet release.
In darkness, hope never takes flight,
It spirals back in prickly light.

So wander forth, let your spirit gleam,
In shadows that cradle each tiny dream.
For where thorns guard the things we find,
True treasures linger, our hearts in kind.

Tapestry of Thorn and Faerie

In the woods where shadows creep,
Thorns entangle dreams that seep.
Faeries dance with glinting light,
Whispers weave into the night.

Beneath the boughs, a secret glade,
Memories linger, softly laid.
Eldritch tunes in breezes blend,
A symphony that will not end.

Ephemeral, the twilight's grace,
Leaves a mark, a fleeting trace.
Bound by fate, the nightingale,
Sings of quests where hearts prevail.

Threads of time in patterns spun,
A dance of thorns, a story begun.
Magic hums in corners lost,
As dreams unfurl, no matter the cost.

Chronicles of a Wistful Thicket

Through thickets deep, a path unwinds,
Where ancient lore in silence binds.
Each rustle tells a tale of yore,
And echoes of what came before.

Mossy stones and winding streams,
Conjure up forgotten dreams.
Creatures whisper soft and low,
In the shadows, secrets grow.

Glimmers of light past branches sway,
Guide the lost who seek their way.
Ink on bark of tales retold,
In soft green hues, the past unfolds.

With every footfall, memories bloom,
Filling the air with sweet perfume.
Time weaves through the leaves it knits,
A tapestry where magic sits.

The Sylvan Chamber of Twinkling Tales

In the sylvan chamber, stars take flight,
Twinkling softly, a wondrous sight.
Stories linger in the air,
With hopes and dreams beyond compare.

Candles flicker with each soft breeze,
Filling hearts with whispered pleas.
A world unfolds in gentle tones,
Crafted by unseen hands and bones.

Squirrels chatter, owls softly hoot,
Nature's song, a sweet pursuit.
In every crease of bark and vine,
Lives a tale, both yours and mine.

Buried deep in shadows cast,
Lies a future forged from the past.
In every glimmer, tales arise,
Carried forth on starlit skies.

Lament of the Gnarled Fables

In the gnarled branches, stories sigh,
Legends linger, never die.
Tales of woe and heart's desire,
Flicker like a dying fire.

With weathered bark and twisted roots,
Echoes stir in whispered toots.
Old as time, these fables dwell,
In the silence, they weave their spell.

Mourn the tales that fade away,
Lost in dusk, they yearn to stay.
Yet in sorrow, wisdom grows,
From every tear a new story flows.

Owls may hoot, and shadows clash,
But every end leads to a flash.
The gnarled fables, dark and deep,
Hold the dreams we dare to keep.

Prologues of the Woodland's Embrace

In the shade where whispers dwell,
Secrets weave a timeless spell.
Leaves in motion dance and glide,
Nature's heart, our souls confide.

Mossy paths where shadows creep,
Silent songs in twilight steep.
Breezes carry tales of yore,
Echoes from the forest floor.

Beneath the boughs of ancient trees,
Golden light sails on the breeze.
Creeping vines and blossoms rare,
Dreams awaken, wander there.

Each footfall stirs the woodland's tale,
In hallowed glades where spirits sail.
Moments cradle, soft and clear,
In every bloom, a whispered cheer.

As twilight falls, the stars ignite,
Guiding lost dreams through the night.
In the woodland's warm embrace,
Our hearts find calm, our fears erase.

The Spines That Sing of Hidden Lore

From ancient stones, the stories pour,
Of battles fought, of distant lore.
Spines of books beneath the stars,
Hold secrets wrapped in shadowed scars.

Each page a map of hallowed ground,
In whispered truths, the past is found.
Chapters woven thick with time,
Echo with a haunting rhyme.

Words like shadows in the night,
Flit through corridors of light.
Guardians of wisdom, steeped in dreams,
Guarding paths of hidden themes.

Through rusted gates and ivy's kiss,
We wander lost in tales of bliss.
Echoes of laughter, tears of pain,
In every line, a heart's refrain.

Let the spines sing soft and low,
While the moon casts its silver glow.
In the silence, lore unfurls,
A tapestry of time in twirls.

Whorled Dreams in the Fairy's Hideaway

In twilight's hush, the fairies play,
Amidst the blooms, they dance and sway.
Whorled dreams spun on gossamer threads,
Cocooned in magic, where hope treads.

Mushroom rings and faerie lights,
Guide our hearts through starry nights.
Laughter mingles with the breeze,
In secret fields, a world of ease.

Petals open to the dawn,
Where gentle spells awaken fawn.
In crystal pools, reflections gleam,
A wondrous thread, our hearts redeem.

Time dissolves in this sweet space,
Where every soul finds their own grace.
Hidden wonders, soft and bright,
Whisper softly into the night.

In the fairy's warm embrace,
Each dream leads us to a place.
Where the ordinary fades away,
To unveil life's ethereal play.

Crown of Twisted Thorn and Grace

Upon the crown of twisted thorn,
Beauty and pain are softly worn.
Grace in struggle, strength in pain,
Life's tapestry weaves joy and disdain.

With petals soft and colors bright,
A reminder of the inner fight.
Through trials faced, the spirit soars,
Each thorn a tale the heart adores.

In every bloom, a truth revealed,\nCourage found, and
wounds healed.
Life's delicate, yet fierce embrace,
Shapes our journey with noble grace.

Beneath the thorns, the roots entwine,
In silent strength, our dreams align.
From tangled briars, roses grow,
In shadows deep, new paths will glow.

The crown we bear, a badge of pride,
A journey embarked, a fate to ride.
Twisted thorns that lace our dreams,
Nurtured by hope's gentle beams.

Thorns Adorned with Celestial Dust

In the quiet glades where shadows weave,
Thorns stand tall, their secrets believe.
Dressed in dust from the stars above,
Each prick a tale of lost love.

Whispers float on the midnight air,
Carrying dreams of those who dare.
Petals flutter, a dance of fate,
Encapsulating a world so great.

Among the thorns, brave hearts will climb,
Searching for jewels, unearthing rhyme.
With every bruise, strength is found,
In silence, the universe surrounds.

Glimmers of hope in the darkest night,
Sparkle softly, catching the light.
Beneath the scrapes, beauty lies,
Awakening spirits, making them rise.

So tread with care where thorns do bloom,
In their embrace, you'll find a room.
To dream, to linger, to softly trust,
For every thorn has its celestial dust.

Glistening Secrets of the Enchanted Thicket

In the heart of the thicket, secrets gleam,
Laced with magic, stitched in a dream.
Fireflies dance through the shimmering night,
Guiding the lost with gentle light.

Whispers of wind tell tales long past,
Of forgotten paths that forever last.
Clever creatures hide in the shade,
Their glistening secrets, a masquerade.

Moss carpets ground, soft and lush,
As time slows down in the twilight hush.
Branches intertwine in a lover's embrace,
Guarding the treasures of this hidden place.

Glimmers of dew on leaves that sway,
Hold stories of hope that won't fade away.
In every droplet, a wish so sweet,
Echoes of hearts that never retreat.

So wander softly through this realm,
Where nature's wonders are at the helm.
The thicket whispers, its spirits alive,
In its glistening secrets, we thrive.

The Tales Beneath the Bristlebark

Beneath the bristlebark, a world concealed,
Woven in shadows, its wonders revealed.
Tangled roots reach deep through the earth,
Cradling whispers of ancient birth.

A fox slips by with a knowing glance,
While in the underbrush, the rabbits dance.
Each rustle and sigh, a story unfolds,
Of quests long ago, brave, yet bold.

In the twilight's glow, secrets unfold,
Tales of chivalry and hearts of gold.
Underneath the bark, dreams softly hum,
Waiting for wonder, awaiting their sum.

The bristle thorns guard their cherished lore,
Of love and loss, but oh, so much more.
Time weaves its magic, steadfast and wise,
As stars pen new fables across the skies.

So linger a while by the bristlebark's side,
Where echoes of stories seek to abide.
In each hidden twist, you might find a spark,
Illuminating dreams beneath the bristlebark.

Echoes of Mischief and Bramble

Through bramble and thicket, mischief does play,
Echoes of laughter fill the light of day.
With every snap of a twig underfoot,
A tale ignites where the wild things scoot.

The sprites and the shadows whisper and tease,
Conducting the symphony swayed by the breeze.
In hidden alcoves where secrets combine,
Bramble weaves magic, both cruel and divine.

With sneaky eyes, the owls observe,
As runners of night keenly observe.
They watch as the moonlight dances and spins,
A luminous silence, where all mischief begins.

As dawn creeps gently, the echoes subside,
But the spirit of mischief remains and will bide.
For in tangled brambles, the wild things still frolic,
In a joyful ruckus, so vibrant, so holic.

So embrace the chaos, the fun and the jest,
In the echoes of bramble, be put to the test.
For life amongst mischief is where we belong,
In the heart of enchantment, we find our song.

Scribbles Beneath Petal and Stem

In gardens where whispers of secrets hide,
Soft petals unfurl, like thoughts that abide.
A dance of the breezes, sweet tales in bloom,
Ink spills from the heart, dispelling the gloom.

Among the green whispers, wild colors unite,
Each stem holds a story, a shy little sprite.
A scribble of laughter, the dance of a bee,
Awakens the magic, in realms yet to see.

The moon casts its glow, where shadows entwine,
In dewdrops that glisten, the stars align.
Beneath every blossom, a dream lies in wait,
In scribbles of nature, we find our true fate.

Winds carry secrets to faraway lands,
As petals are brushed by invisible hands.
Each crease tells a story, old whispers, anew,
In the language of flowers, our souls can break through.

So linger a moment, beneath this soft shade,
Where scribbles of life, in the twilight, cascade.
In the arms of the earth, our hearts shall take flight,
In the garden of scribbles, we'll dance through the night.

Luminous Spheres in the Thicket Night

In the thicket where shadows weave tales of old,
Luminous spheres cast a glow, soft and bold.
They twinkle like wishes, so fragile, so bright,
Guiding the wanderers through the tapestry night.

Each orb tells a story, of dreams long ago,
Of lovers and legends, of laughter and woe.
They float on the breezes, like secrets they share,
Illuminating paths, with the promise of care.

As crickets compose their night symphony sweet,
The spheres pirouette, with a graceful heartbeat.
In the hush of the dusk, where the magic takes flight,
These luminous spirits embrace the night's light.

Through the thicket they dance, in a whimsical spell,
Drawing all hearts to their luminous well.
With each gentle flicker, they beckon and call,
To wander the wilds, where shadows enthrall.

So follow the glow, through the dense, darkened trees,
With courage and wonder, ride the night's gentle breeze.
For in luminous spheres, our dreams shall ignite,
A world full of magic, unveiling the night.

Stalk Stories of the Woodland Realm

In woodland realms where the tall trees abide,
Stalk stories whisper from roots that divide.
Echoes of laughter, of creatures and dreams,
In the shadowy depths, where sunlight redeems.

A knot in the trunk holds a tale of the years,
Of storms weathered, and of hidden tears.
The rustle of leaves sings of journeys unknown,
Each stalk bears witness, in green woven tones.

Through thickets and glades, where the wildflowers sway,

Secrets lay scattered in a delicate spray.
In the arms of the forest, where whispers unite,
Stalk stories unfold, beneath shimmers of light.

From mushrooms that flourish to ferns that entwine,
Every soft sound is a chapter divine.
The forest, a storyteller, ancient and wise,
In the echoing silence, the heart learns to rise.

So wander the paths, let the stories unfold,
In the woodland's embrace, where the brave turn bold.
For in stalks of each tree, in the moss and the mire,
Lie tales of resilience, of hope, and of fire.

Grove Echoes: A Ballad of Branches

In the grove where the branches entwine and sway,
Whispers of nature in soft, breezy play.
Each leaf has a voice, a melody sweet,
While echoes of sunlight dance down at our feet.

The branches reach upward, embracing the sky,
Inviting the stars to softly reply.
As twilight descends, with its shimmering glow,
The grove comes alive, as the cool breezes flow.

A ballad of ages, sung softly by trees,
Rustles the leaves, sways the boughs with ease.
In the heart of the grove where the ancients reside,
The echoes of stories in shadows do glide.

With every sweet rustle, a history breathes,
From the roots to the branches, the wisdom reprieves.
In the cover of dusk, where the quiet ones roam,
The grove sings a ballad, calling all hearts home.

So linger awhile, let the soft breezes tell,
Of moments enchanted, where memories dwell.
In the echoes of branches, find solace and grace,
In the grove's tender embrace, our spirits find place.

Lightfall

In whispers soft, the dawn awakes,
Through misty veils, the sunlight breaks.
A golden hue on leaves aglow,
Dancing shadows in a gentle flow.

The forest breathes, a living spell,
In every corner, secrets dwell.
The light cascades like silver streams,
Awakening the world of dreams.

Fairies flutter, on wings of hope,
They weave their stories, help us cope.
With every flutter, a tale is spun,
In the heart of light, our journeys run.

Oh, hear the call of light's embrace,
In every leaf, a hidden grace.
As day unfolds, the magic swells,
In whispered tones, the forest dwells.

A tapestry of gold and green,
Where every moment's yet unseen.
In strands of time, the past runs deep,
As lightfall beckons, dreams we keep.

Elfin Thorns

In shadows deep where thorns entwine,
The elves weave magic, darkly fine.
Among the brambles, tales do hide,
Of lost enchantments, deep inside.

Their laughter echoes through the night,
In moonlit glades, where hearts take flight.
With silver hair and eyes so bright,
They guard the dreams that spark the light.

Beneath the thorns, a secret lies,
Where whispered wishes never die.
In tangled roots, the past's refrain,
Keeps hopeful hearts from chasing pain.

Yet beware the touch of fading charms,
For in their beauty, danger warms.
A thorn may prickle, yet it binds,
The spirit's quest in hidden finds.

Elfin thorns and shadows blend,
In realms where magic knows no end.
With every step, a choice we make,
As dreams intertwine with hearts that break.

Enigma of the Gnarled Woods

In gnarled woods where shadows play,
An enigma waits to guide the way.
With twisted roots and bark so old,
The stories linger, yet untold.

The whispering trees hold secrets deep,
Of timeless oaths that forest keep.
In knotted branches, wishes glide,
While shadows dance in nature's stride.

A haunting melody fills the air,
The woods beckon, with a gentle care.
Through tangled paths, the curious roam,
In this embrace, the heart finds home.

The echoes call, a siren's song,
In the heart of woods, we all belong.
With every step, a mystery grows,
In gnarled embrace, our spirit knows.

An enigma wrapped in nature's arms,
Enchanting souls with hidden charms.
For every shadow, a light will beam,
In gnarled woods, we chase the dream.

Tangle of Tales Among Forest Spirits

In moonlit glades where spirits roam,
A tangle of tales finds its home.
With voices soft as evening breeze,
They share their lore among the trees.

Each leaf a whisper, each branch a sigh,
As stories build and times pass by.
With playful giggles and knowing grins,
The spirits weave where magic begins.

From ancient roots to skies above,
Their tales speak of loss and love.
In every shadow, a passage waits,
As forest spirits open gates.

A dance of fables, old and new,
In twilight's glow, they take their cue.
With every heartbeat, legends twine,
In tangled woods, our souls align.

So listen close, and hear the song,
In forest halls where we belong.
For in this tangle of dreams and light,
The stories blossom through the night.

Under the Veil of Verdant Mystery

In the heart where shadows play,
The whispers of the leaves sway,
A tapestry of emerald hue,
Where secrets breathe and dreams renew.

Beneath the boughs of ancient grace,
The sunlight dances, soft embrace,
Each petal gazes, wide and bright,
A treasure hidden in the light.

Crickets sing a tune so light,
While fireflies paint the veil of night,
In twilight's grasp, all fears disperse,
The forest weaves a gentle verse.

With every rustle, stories stir,
As time slips by, a mystic blur,
From roots entwined to branches high,
A world awaits beneath the sky.

In silence deep, the magics weave,
In every sigh, in dreams we cleave,
For nature's heart, a wondrous spree,
Unfolds the truths we long to see.

Fantasies Woven in Stalwart Stems

Among the thickets wild and free,
Adventures dance, as bold as glee,
With every stalk, a story grows,
In whispers where the wild heart glows.

From daisy's crown to rose's breath,
Life blooms anew, defying death,
Each petal's tale is spun with care,
In tangled dreams that linger there.

Through all the seasons, bright and fair,
A symphony of scents and air,
With colors vivid, fiercely bright,
In gardens where the stars ignite.

The daisies nod with soft delight,
As shadows lengthen, day to night,
In every root, an echo sings,
Of magic spun on silken wings.

So let your spirit roam and soar,
Through blooms that beckon evermore,
For in each stem, a dream persists,
A truth in life that can't be missed.

Ethereal Touches in the Woodland Whisper

The woods awake with muffled sighs,
As starlight spills from velvet skies,
With every blink, the shadows shift,
A tapestry of dreams they gift.

Each leaf a page, each branch a tale,
In nature's hush, the spirits sail,
Through glimmers bright in twilight's glow,
To realms where only dreamers go.

The owls they call, the crickets chirp,
As time flows gentle like a burp,
In every rustle, peace enfolds,
The secrets of the night are told.

Moonbeams weave through foliage thick,
With silver threads, they craft and pick,
A world where magic takes its stand,
In whispered tales that nature planned.

So wander deep where spirits dwell,
And follow scents that cast their spell,
For in the heart of whispered words,
The dreams of night are softly heard.

Blooming Curiosities Under Dewy Mist

Awake and gaze at morning's grace,
With frosted jewels on nature's face,
The world unfolds with gilded thread,
A tapestry of life widespread.

In meadows bright where wonders bloom,
Each petal glows, dispelling gloom,
With every droplet, secrets gleam,
In dewy mists, we chase a dream.

The blossoms whisper tales of yore,
Of summer's warmth and winter's lore,
With fragile forms that bend and sway,
A dance of colors bold and gay.

As morning light begins to rise,
The playful shadows start to disguise,
A flourish here, a twirl so swift,
In nature's heart, our dreams uplift.

So venture forth where wonders lie,
With every step, let spirits fly,
For in the bloom beneath the mist,
Are stories held in nature's fist.

www.ingramcontent.com/pod-product-compliance
Lightning Source LLC
Chambersburg PA
CBHW051946220125
20712CB00003B/128